God Created

GOD CREATED

Text copyright © 2003 Mark Francisco Bozzuti-Jones. Illustrations copyright © 2003 Jui Ishida. All rights reserved. Except for brief quotations in critical articles or reviews, no part of this book may be reproduced in any manner without prior written permission from the publisher. Write to: Permissions, Augsburg Fortress, Box 1209, Minneapolis, MN 55440.

Large-quantity purchases or custom editions of this book are available at a discount from the publisher. For more information, contact the sales department at Augsburg Fortress, Publishers, 1-800-328-4648, or write to: Sales Director, Augsburg Fortress, Publishers, P.O. Box 1209, Minneapolis, MN 55440-1209.

ISBN 0-8066-4568-7

Cover and book design by Michelle L. N. Cook

The paper used in this publication meets the minimum requirements of American National Standard for Information Sciences—Permanence of Paper for Printed Library Materials, ANSI Z329.48-1984. ⊖ ™

Manufactured in Singapore

07   06   05   04   4   5   6   7   8   9   10

God Created

BY MARK FRANCISCO BOZZUTI-JONES

ILLUSTRATED BY JUI ISHIDA

Augsburg Books
Bringing Families Together
for Children & Families

To Kathy Bozzuti-Jones and

Mark Anthony Francisco Bozzuti-Jones II,

who teach me the blessings of God's creation

In the beginning . . .

Silence. Spirit.

God created everything.

The heavens,
the skies,
the air,
the rain,
the water,

the earth.

God created men, women,
and children all over the earth.

Seeds,

    plants,

and trees all over the earth;

lions,
giraffes,
tigers,
and elephants,

cats,
dogs,
horses,

and bears—

all over the earth.

God created all these

and much more,

and much more,

so much more.

God created birds,

insects,

fishes, whales,

plants in the waters,

the river,

the pond,

the sea,

the ocean caressing the land.

God created all these

and much more,

and much more,

so much more.

God created

words and meanings,

language and stories,

shouting and singing,
songs, poems, riddles,
sound and quiet.

God created all these things:

questions, answers,

faith, love, hope,

and much more.

God created tears and laughter,
smiles,
frowns,
winces,
hugs and friendships, too.

God created all these
and much more,
and much more,

so much more.

God created peace, stillness,

days for waiting,

dreams,

desires,

wishes.

God created the beginning.
God created the middle.
God created the end

of all things
with all things
for all things.

God created life—
all that is seen and unseen.

God created life—
love from God
that will never end.

God created all these

and much more,

and much more,

so much more.

Yes, it is true:
All we can hear,
taste, touch, see,
be, or imagine—

God created all these
and much more,

and much more,

so much more . . .

God created you.